Author's Note:

If this book resonates with you and can help others, feel free to recommend it or talk about it on your social media. May these ideas reach those who need them. Thank you!

Link to access Reginald Rivers' books on amazon.com
https://www.amazon.com.br/s?k=reginald+rivers

Or type "Reginald Rivers" (in parentheses) into the search bar on amazon.com.

Title: *Artificial Intelligence*
Subtitle: *Unveiling the Future*
Author: *Reginald Rivers*

Table of Contents

Chapter 1: Introduction

- What is Artificial Intelligence?

- The Importance of AI in the Modern World

Chapter 2: The History and Evolution of AI

- Origins and Development

- Major Milestones in AI History

Chapter 3: Fundamentals of Artificial Intelligence

- Basic Concepts and Definitions

- Machine Learning and Deep Learning

- Neural Networks and AI Algorithms

Chapter 4: Practical Applications of Artificial Intelligence

- Autonomous Vehicles – Israel's Iron Dome
- Aviation – Space Research – Image Creation
- Digital Marketing – The Defense Industry

Chapter 5: AI in Healthcare

- AI-Assisted Medical Diagnostics
- Pharmaceutical Research and Drug Discovery
- Healthcare Management

Chapter 6: AI in Education

- Personalized Learning
- Assessment Tools
- AI as a Teaching Tool

Chapter 7: AI and the Environment

- Monitoring and Managing Natural Resources
- Climate Change
- Sustainability

Chapter 8: The Social and Ethical Impact of AI

- Privacy and Security

- Algorithmic Bias and Fairness

- Impact on Employment and the Economy

Chapter 9: Technical Challenges and the Future of AI

- Current Limitations

- Explainable and Transparent AI

- Future Prospects

Chapter 10: AI and the Law

- Regulations and Policies

- Intellectual Property

- AI in Litigation

Chapter 11: Human-Machine Interaction

- Brain-Computer Interface

- Social Robotics

- Ethics in Automation

Chapter 12: Conclusion

- Final Reflections

- The Future of AI

Chapter 13: Appendices

- Glossary of AI Terms

- References and Further Reading

Chapter 1: *Introduction*

What is Artificial Intelligence?

Artificial Intelligence (AI) is a branch of computer science focused on creating machines capable of performing tasks that typically require human intelligence. This includes activities such as learning, reasoning, problem-solving, perception, understanding, and using natural language.

Since its inception in the 1940s and 1950s, AI has evolved significantly. Originally, it aimed to simulate specific aspects of human intelligence. Today, it encompasses a variety of sophisticated technologies, such as machine learning, neural networks, natural language processing (NLP), and robotics.

AI is classified into two main types: Narrow AI (or Weak AI) and General AI (or Strong AI). Narrow AI is designed to perform specific tasks, such as virtual assistants and recommendation systems. General AI, on the other hand, remains a theoretical goal and represents a form of intelligence that could perform any intellectual task a human can.

AI applications are everywhere, from email filtering and product recommendations to advanced medical diagnostics and self-driving cars. The technology has the potential to revolutionize countless fields and industries.

However, AI development also brings

significant ethical and practical challenges, including concerns about privacy, security, algorithmic bias, and its impact on the job market. These issues are fundamental to guiding AI's future in a responsible and beneficial manner.

The Importance of AI in the Modern World
Artificial Intelligence (AI) has become a fundamental driving force in the modern world, impacting nearly every aspect of contemporary life. Its influence extends from optimizing business operations to improving quality of life

and public health. Below are some key aspects of its importance.

Innovation and Business Efficiency

In the business sector, AI is revolutionizing how companies operate. Machine learning

algorithms are used to analyze market data, optimize supply chains, personalize customer experiences, and automate repetitive tasks. This not only increases efficiency but also opens new possibilities for innovation and business

strategies.

Advances in Healthcare

AI plays a crucial role in healthcare, from developing new drugs to providing more accurate and personalized diagnoses. AI systems are being employed to analyze large medical datasets, leading to significant

discoveries and more effective treatments for a variety of conditions.

Impact on Education

In education, AI offers opportunities for

personalized learning and access to high-quality educational resources. Intelligent systems can adapt teaching materials to each student's pace and learning style, making education more accessible and effective.

Improved Quality of Life

For the general public, AI enhances quality of life in various ways. From smart personal assistants that simplify daily tasks to recommendation systems that help us find relevant content and products, AI makes many aspects of daily life more convenient and personalized.

Challenges and Responsibility

With all this potential come great

responsibilities. It is essential to address the ethical questions AI raises, such as data privacy, algorithmic bias, and its impact on employment. The challenge is to ensure that

AI's benefits are distributed fairly and that its systems are transparent, secure, and ethical.

Chapter 2: *The History and Evolution of AI*

Origins and Development

The journey of Artificial Intelligence (AI) is both fascinating and complex, beginning long before modern computers and algorithms. Let's explore its origins and development up to the present day.

Philosophical and Mathematical Roots

The idea of thinking machines dates back to ancient times, with philosophers and scientists speculating about the nature of intelligence and the possibility of replicating it artificially. However, the formal birth of AI as a scientific field occurred in the 20th century. Mathematicians and thinkers like Alan Turing, with his famous "Turing Test," laid the theoretical foundations for what would become AI.

The Dartmouth Conference: The Birth of a Field

The year 1956, marked by the Dartmouth Conference organized by John McCarthy and others, is considered the official birth of AI as a formal discipline. This event brought together brilliant minds to discuss and explore the idea that machines could not only calculate but also learn and adapt.

Decades of Growth and 'AI Winters'

Since Dartmouth, AI has gone through phases of optimism and development, interspersed with periods of stagnation and disillusionment, known as "AI winters." In the 1960s and 1970s, initial enthusiasm led to significant advances but also to unrealistic expectations, which were not met due to the technological limitations of the time.

The Machine Learning Era

The resurgence of AI began in the 1980s and gained momentum in the 1990s with the advent of machine learning. Access to large datasets and a significant increase in computational power allowed algorithms to learn and improve from examples, paving the way for practical applications on a large scale.

Recent Advances and Modern AI

Today, AI is an undeniable reality, driven by advances in areas like deep neural networks, natural language processing, and autonomous systems. It is redefining industries, creating new opportunities and challenges, and continuing to evolve at an accelerated pace.

Major Milestones in AI History

The history of Artificial Intelligence is marked by several significant events and revolutionary innovations. These milestones not only showcase technological progress but also reflect the growing understanding of AI's complexity and potential.

1950 – Turing Test: Proposed by Alan Turing, this test was one of the first attempts to define and evaluate machine intelligence. A machine could be considered "intelligent" if it could mimic human behavior to the point of being indistinguishable from a human in conversation.

1956 – Dartmouth Conference: This event is often cited as the official birth of AI as a formal field of study. Participants, including John McCarthy and Marvin Minsky, established AI as a legitimate academic goal.

1966 – ELIZA: Developed by Joseph

Weizenbaum, ELIZA was one of the first programs capable of processing natural language, functioning as a "psychotherapist" and marking a significant breakthrough in human-computer interaction.

1974-1980 – First AI Winter: Characterized by a lack of funding and reduced interest in AI, primarily due to inflated and unmet expectations.

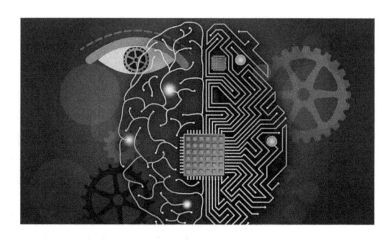

1980 – AI Revival with Expert Systems: The 1980s saw an AI revival, driven by the success of expert systems—programs capable of making decisions in specific fields like medicine and geology.

1997 – IBM's Deep Blue Defeats Garry Kasparov: A significant milestone in AI, where a computer defeated a world chess champion for the first time, demonstrating major advances in AI's ability to solve complex problems.

2000s – Machine Learning and Big Data: With the advent of the internet and the explosion of digital data, machine learning became a crucial tool for analyzing large datasets, leading to significant advances in areas from speech recognition to content personalization.

2010s – Rise of Deep Neural Networks: The introduction and refinement of deep neural networks led to notable improvements in tasks like image recognition and machine translation, ushering in the era of "deep AI."

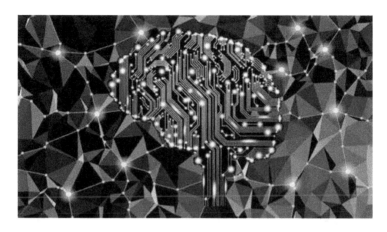

2016 – DeepMind's AlphaGo Defeats Lee Sedol: This event marked a remarkable breakthrough in AI. AlphaGo, an AI program specialized in the game of Go, defeated a world champion, overcoming one of the most complex challenges in strategy and intuition.

Chapter 3: *Fundamentals of Artificial Intelligence*

Basic Concepts and Definitions

Understanding the fundamentals of Artificial Intelligence (AI) begins with defining some basic concepts and key terms that form the backbone of this fascinating and ever-evolving field.

Artificial Intelligence (AI): In its broadest sense, AI refers to the ability of a machine or system to mimic human intelligence. This includes the ability to learn, reason, solve problems, perceive the environment, and even interact using natural language.

Machine Learning: A subfield of AI, machine learning is the process by which computer systems use algorithms and data to learn and improve their performance on a specific task. It is based on the idea that systems can learn from data, identify patterns, and make decisions with minimal human intervention.

Deep Learning: A subset of machine learning, deep learning uses artificial neural networks with multiple layers (deep neural networks) to simulate the brain's information processing and learning patterns. It is fundamental in complex applications like speech and image recognition.

Neural Networks: Inspired by the biological neural networks of the human brain, neural networks in AI are systems of interconnected algorithms that work together to process data, identify patterns, and aid in decision-making.

AI Algorithms: An AI algorithm is a set of rules and instructions that an AI system follows to perform tasks, solve problems, and make decisions. Algorithms can range from simple decision rules to complex mathematical calculations.

Natural Language Processing (NLP): An area of AI focused on enabling computers to read, understand, and interpret human language. NLP is key to creating systems that can interact naturally with users, such as virtual assistants and chatbots.

Automation and Robotics: While not all automation or robotics involves AI, integrating AI systems into robots and industrial automation is expanding capabilities and applications in these fields, from manufacturing to household tasks.

Machine Learning and Deep Learning

Within the fundamentals of Artificial Intelligence, two concepts stand out for their importance and impact: Machine Learning and Deep Learning. Both represent crucial techniques that enable machines to learn and perform tasks intelligently.

Machine Learning

Machine Learning is the heart of modern AI. It is a technique that allows machines to learn from data and improve their performance on a specific task. The core idea is that systems can learn and adapt without explicit instructions, identifying patterns and making data-driven decisions.

Types of Machine Learning:

- **Supervised Learning:** Algorithms are trained on labeled datasets and learn to predict outcomes from that data.

- **Unsupervised Learning:** Algorithms analyze and group unlabeled data, uncovering hidden patterns or intrinsic structures.

- **Reinforcement Learning:** Algorithms learn to make optimized decisions through trial and error, receiving rewards or penalties.

Deep Learning

Deep Learning is a subfield of Machine Learning based on artificial neural networks with multiple layers. These networks are designed to mimic the way the human brain processes data and patterns. Deep Learning is particularly effective for identifying patterns in large datasets, making it ideal for applications like speech recognition, computer vision, and machine

translation.

Types of Deep Learning Networks:

- **Convolutional Neural Networks**

  (CNNs): Primarily used for image processing tasks, such as facial recognition and medical image analysis.

- **Recurrent Neural Networks**

  (RNNs): Suitable for handling sequential data, like text or audio, and used in machine translation and speech recognition.

Interconnection Between Machine Learning and Deep Learning

Although Deep Learning is a specialization within Machine Learning, it stands out for its ability to process and learn from vast amounts of data more efficiently and deeply. This results in enhanced performance and accuracy in complex tasks, often surpassing other Machine Learning methods.

Neural Networks and AI Algorithms

Neural Networks

Neural networks are one of the central pillars of Artificial Intelligence, particularly in Machine Learning and Deep Learning. Inspired by the structure and function of the human brain, neural networks are systems of algorithms designed to recognize patterns and interpret data.

Structure of Neural Networks: A typical neural network consists of nodes, known as artificial neurons, organized in layers. There is an input layer, one or more hidden layers, and an output layer. Each neuron in a layer is connected to multiple neurons in the next layer, forming a network of interconnections.

Functioning: Neural networks work by being fed large amounts of data. They learn to perform specific tasks by assigning varying weights to inputs and gradually adjusting these weights based on errors made during task execution.

Applications: They are widely used in various applications, such as facial recognition, medical diagnostics, market trend prediction, and much more.

AI Algorithms

AI algorithms are programmed instructions that guide data analysis and decision-making within AI systems. They range from simple classification algorithms to complex deep learning systems.

Types of AI Algorithms:

- **Classification Algorithms:** Used to categorize data into different groups.

- **Regression Algorithms:** Used to predict continuous values, such as weather forecasts or stock prices.

- **Clustering Algorithms:** Involve grouping similar data, such as customer segmentation for marketing.

- **Neural Networks and Deep Learning Algorithms:** For more complex tasks and analysis of large datasets.

Importance of Algorithms in AI: Choosing the right algorithm is crucial, as it determines how effectively an AI task is performed. The right algorithm can mean the difference between an efficient and an ineffective AI model.

Continuing with the book, we move to **Chapter 4: "Practical Applications of Artificial Intelligence,"** covering the sections **"Autonomous**

Vehicles" and **"Israel's Iron Dome."** Here's the text for these parts:

Chapter 4: *Practical Applications of Artificial Intelligence*

Autonomous Vehicles

AI is revolutionizing the automotive industry through the development of self-driving cars. These vehicles use a combination of sensors, cameras, radar, and AI to navigate and drive without human intervention.

Autonomous Driving Technology: AI in self-driving cars involves processing vast amounts of data in real time to make driving decisions. This includes identifying objects on the road, assessing traffic conditions, and predicting potential hazards.

Benefits: Autonomous vehicles have the potential to reduce accidents caused by human error, improve traffic efficiency, and provide greater mobility for people unable to drive.

Challenges and Development: Large-scale mplementation of self-driving cars faces significant challenges, including safety concerns, regulations, and public acceptance.

Israel's Iron Dome

Israel's Iron Dome is a notable example of AI application in defense and security. This missile defense system is designed to intercept and destroy short-range rockets and artillery shells fired at populated areas.

AI and Defense: AI in the Iron Dome enables rapid analysis of radar data to assess the threat posed by an incoming projectile and determine the best response. The system calculates the projectile's likely trajectory and decides whether to intercept it based on criteria like the predicted impact area.

Impact and Efficiency: The system has demonstrated remarkable effectiveness in protecting civilian areas from rocket attacks, saving countless lives. Its ability to make quick, precise decisions under high-pressure situations exemplifies AI's potential in military and defense applications.

Ethical Considerations and Future: The use of AI in defense systems like the Iron Dome also raises important ethical questions, including accountability for automatically made decisions and the future of automated warfare.

Aviation

AI is transforming the aviation industry, improving safety, efficiency, and customer experience. Applications range from aircraft maintenance enhancements to in-flight assistance and air traffic control operations.

Predictive Maintenance: Using AI and data analysis, airlines can predict maintenance issues before they occur, reducing delays and costs.

Intelligent Flight Assistants: AI-based systems assist pilots during flights, providing real-time information and analytics to optimize routes and save fuel.

Air Traffic Management: AI is also used to manage air traffic more efficiently, improving safety and reducing congestion in airspace.

Space Research

AI plays a crucial role in space exploration and research. From processing vast amounts of astronomical data to operating probes and rovers on other planets, AI is expanding the horizons of space exploration.

Space Data Analysis: AI is used to process and analyze data from telescopes and space probes, helping to identify patterns and phenomena that would be difficult for humans to detect.

Autonomous Rovers on Mars: Vehicles like NASA's Perseverance rover use AI to navigate autonomously on the Martian surface, making real-time decisions about where to go and which samples to collect.

Image Creation

AI is revolutionizing image creation in fields like art, design, and entertainment. Through advanced techniques, it's possible to generate realistic images and create visual content efficiently and innovatively.

Artistic Image Generation: AI-based software can create original artwork, learning styles from famous painters or generating entirely new visuals.

Visual Effects in Films and Games: AI is also being used to create realistic visual effects in movies and games, reducing production time and costs.

Image Editing and Restoration: AI

algorithms assist in photo and video editing, from automatic color and lighting adjustments to restoring old images.

Digital Marketing

AI is revolutionizing digital marketing, enabling more personalized, efficient, and data-driven strategies.

Personalization: AI analyzes consumer data to provide personalized recommendations and relevant content, enhancing the customer experience.

Campaign Optimization: AI algorithms can optimize advertising campaigns in real time, adapting to changes in consumer behavior and market trends.

Predictive Analytics: AI is used to predict future consumer trends and behavior, allowing businesses to anticipate market needs.

Chatbots and Customer Support:

AI-powered chatbots provide quick and personalized customer assistance, improving engagement and satisfaction.

The Defense Industry

AI also has significant applications in the defense industry, bringing both advancements and ethical challenges.

Autonomous Weapon Systems: AI is being integrated into weapon systems, enabling autonomous operations. This includes drones capable of carrying out reconnaissance and attack missions without human intervention.

Cybersecurity Defense: AI plays a crucial role in cybersecurity defense, detecting and responding to security threats faster and more efficiently than traditional methods.

Intelligence Analysis: AI algorithms analyze vast amounts of intelligence data, aiding in threat identification and strategic decision-making.

Ethical Issues and Regulation: The use of AI in the defense industry raises important ethical questions, including accountability for decisions made by autonomous systems and the need for international regulation.

Chapter 5: *AI in Healthcare*

AI-Assisted Medical Diagnostics

The application of Artificial Intelligence in healthcare is revolutionizing how medical diagnostics are performed, offering precision, efficiency, and new capabilities that were previously unimaginable.

Medical Image Analysis: One of the most significant uses of AI in medicine is in analyzing medical images, such as X-rays, MRIs, and CT scans. AI algorithms, especially those based on deep learning, can identify subtle patterns in images that might escape the human eye. This is particularly useful for early diagnosis of diseases like cancer, heart conditions, and neurological disorders.

Disease Prediction and Prevention: AI is also used to predict the likelihood of patients developing certain conditions, enabling more effective preventive interventions. For example, algorithms can analyze medical history, genetic data, and lifestyle factors to assess the risk of diseases like diabetes and various cancers.

Clinical Decision Support: AI systems provide decision support to doctors, combining medical knowledge with patient-specific data to offer personalized treatment recommendations. This improves diagnostic accuracy and treatment effectiveness.

Telemedicine and Remote Diagnostics: AI

enables remote diagnostics and consultations through telemedicine, expanding access to quality healthcare, especially in remote or underserved regions.

Challenges and Ethical

Considerations: Despite the benefits, using AI in medical diagnostics presents challenges, including the need for large training datasets, ensuring patient data privacy, and effectively integrating AI into clinical workflows.

Additionally, ethical issues related to the reliability and interpretability of AI-driven decisions are important considerations.

Pharmaceutical Research and Drug Discovery

Artificial Intelligence is playing a revolutionary role in pharmaceutical research and drug discovery, accelerating treatment development and significantly reducing time and costs.

Compound Screening: AI can quickly analyze and predict the efficacy of millions of chemical compounds, identifying potential candidates for new drugs. This is especially useful for finding treatments for complex and rare diseases.

Personalized Drug Development: Using genetic data and biomarkers, AI is facilitating the creation of personalized drugs. This approach allows for treatments that are more effective for specific individuals or patient groups based on their unique genetics and biological characteristics.

Modeling and Simulation: AI algorithms can model and simulate how compounds interact with biological targets, helping predict a drug's efficacy and potential side effects even before clinical trials.

Clinical Trial Optimization: AI is also transforming how clinical trials are conducted, from participant selection to real-time monitoring and analysis of results. This includes using algorithms to identify the most suitable candidates for trials and to track and analyze data in real time.

Challenges and Regulation: Despite its potential, AI in drug discovery faces challenges, including the need for high-quality datasets and issues related to algorithm validation and regulation. Additionally, there is a growing need for collaboration between data scientists, biologists, and pharmacologists to ensure effective drug development.

Healthcare Management

Artificial Intelligence is transforming healthcare management, improving operational efficiency, patient care quality, and clinical decision-making.

Patient Data Management: AI helps manage and analyze large volumes of patient data, including electronic health records, lab results, and treatment histories. This enables a more comprehensive view of the patient, aiding in informed clinical decisions and personalized care.

Hospital Resource Optimization: AI

algorithms optimize resource allocation in hospitals, such as bed management, surgery scheduling, and staff distribution. This improves operational efficiency and reduces costs.

Remote Patient Monitoring: AI enables

remote patient monitoring, particularly useful for managing chronic conditions. Smart devices and apps can collect real-time health data, alerting healthcare providers to changes that require attention.

Outbreak Prediction and Public Health

Trends: AI can analyze public health data to predict disease outbreaks and health trends, enabling proactive and efficient responses from public health authorities.

Clinical Decision Support: AI-based decision support systems integrate clinical data, medical research, and guidelines to provide recommendations to healthcare professionals. This aids in identifying treatment options and reducing medical errors.

Challenges and Ethical

Considerations: Despite advancements,

implementing AI in healthcare management faces challenges like integration with existing systems, ensuring patient data privacy and security, and guaranteeing equitable access to AI-enhanced care.

Chapter 6: *AI in Education*

Personalized Learning

The application of Artificial Intelligence in education is opening new pathways for personalized learning, offering educational experiences tailored to each student's individual needs.

Adaptive Learning Systems: AI can create adaptive learning systems that adjust content and pace based on a student's progress and needs. This is achieved by analyzing how students interact with materials, identifying strengths, weaknesses, and preferred learning styles.

Personalized Feedback and Assessment: AI algorithms provide instant, personalized feedback to students. They can evaluate assignments and exams, highlighting areas for improvement and recommending additional resources or practice exercises.

Intelligent Learning Platforms: These platforms use AI to recommend courses, reading materials, and activities based on students' preferences and learning history. This not only enhances the learning experience but also encourages continuous student engagement.

Virtual Teaching Assistants: AI enables the development of virtual teaching assistants that can answer student questions, help organize tasks, and even facilitate discussions in online forums.

Challenges and Opportunities: While AI in education offers opportunities to personalize and enhance learning, it also presents challenges, such as ensuring equitable access to these technologies and addressing concerns about student data privacy. Additionally, it's crucial to maintain a balance between technology and the irreplaceable role of human educators.

Assessment Tools

The implementation of Artificial Intelligence in education extends beyond teaching to assessment tools, revolutionizing how student performance is measured and analyzed.

Automated Assessment: AI enables automated assessment of student responses, including multiple-choice tests and written answers. Advanced algorithms can evaluate not only accuracy but also the quality of reasoning, clarity of expression, and creativity.

Learning Pattern Analysis: Through data analysis, AI tools can identify patterns in student performance over time. This helps detect areas where students may consistently struggle, allowing for more targeted and effective interventions.

Personalized and Constructive

Feedback: Beyond evaluation, AI provides detailed, personalized feedback to students. This can include suggestions on how to improve in specific areas, recommendations for additional resources, or study strategies.

Plagiarism Detection and Academic

Integrity: AI-based tools are increasingly used to detect plagiarism and ensure academic integrity. They can analyze text and compare it to a vast database to identify potential cases of copying or improper use of material.

Challenges and Limitations: While AI-powered assessment tools offer many advantages, they also present challenges. Issues like algorithmic bias, accuracy in evaluating complex responses, and the need for human oversight are ongoing concerns. Additionally, over-reliance on technology may undervalue subjective and qualitative aspects of education that are difficult to quantify.

AI as a Teaching Tool

Artificial Intelligence is emerging as a powerful teaching tool, transforming the educational experience for both teachers and students.

AI-Based Teaching Assistants: AI is enabling the development of virtual teaching assistants that can help teachers with administrative tasks, such as preparing teaching materials and organizing lesson plans. They can also assist in evaluating student progress and identifying areas needing additional attention.

Personalized Educational Content: AI algorithms can create personalized educational content, adapting to each student's skill level and learning style. This includes tailoring lessons, exercises, and teaching materials to meet individual needs, making learning more effective and engaging.

Interaction and Engagement: AI tools can facilitate student interaction and engagement, offering interactive platforms that include educational games, simulations, and hands-on activities. This can be particularly beneficial in online learning environments, where direct interaction with teachers and peers may be limited.

Support for Students with Special Needs: AI has the potential to provide personalized support to students with special educational needs. For example, AI programs can be designed to assist students with dyslexia in reading and writing or offer adapted resources for students with different learning styles.

Professional Development for Teachers: AI can also be a valuable tool for teachers' professional development, offering insights and feedback on their teaching practices. This can include guidance on improving content delivery and effectively engaging students.

Challenges and Ethical

Considerations: While AI as a teaching tool offers many opportunities, it also brings challenges. Issues related to data privacy, over-reliance on technology, and the need to balance automated teaching with human interaction are important concerns. Additionally, it's essential that technology is used to complement and enrich teaching, not to replace the valuable interaction between teachers and students.

Chapter 7: AI and the Environment

Monitoring and Managing Natural Resources

Artificial Intelligence plays a fundamental role in monitoring and managing natural resources, contributing significantly to environmental sustainability.

Environmental Monitoring: AI is used to monitor ecosystems and natural habitats, utilizing data from satellites, remote sensors, and other sources. These systems can detect changes in vegetation patterns, water levels, air quality, and other environmental indicators, helping to identify deforestation, soil degradation, or pollution early and accurately.

Water and Agriculture Management: In agriculture, AI helps optimize water use and increase crop efficiency. Algorithms can predict water demand based on weather conditions, soil type, and other factors, enabling more sustainable water use. Similarly, AI can help identify plant diseases and suggest the best treatment strategies.

Biodiversity Conservation: AI algorithms are used in biodiversity conservation to analyze animal migration patterns, monitor at-risk populations, and identify critical conservation areas. This enables more effective interventions to protect endangered species.

Natural Disaster Prediction and Mitigation: AI contributes to predicting and mitigating natural disasters, such as floods, wildfires, and storms. Algorithms can analyze vast amounts of meteorological and geographical data to forecast events more accurately and provide early warnings, saving lives and reducing damage.

Challenges and Opportunities: While AI offers many opportunities for environmental management, it also presents challenges, including the need for high-quality data and the integration of AI insights into public policy and management practices. Additionally, it's vital to ensure that AI solutions are implemented ethically and sustainably.

Climate Change

Artificial Intelligence (AI) is emerging as a powerful tool in the fight against climate change, offering new ways to understand, mitigate, and adapt to its impacts.

Climate Modeling and Simulation: AI algorithms are being used to improve climate modeling and simulation, enabling more accurate and detailed predictions. These models help scientists and policymakers better understand the effects of climate change and assess the effectiveness of various mitigation strategies.

Analysis of Large Environmental

Datasets: AI can process and analyze massive volumes of environmental data from sources like satellites, ocean sensors, and weather stations. This allows for the identification of patterns and trends that would be difficult to detect manually, such as subtle temperature changes, CO2 levels, and glacier melting patterns.

Energy and Resource Optimization: AI helps optimize energy and resource use, thereby reducing greenhouse gas emissions. This includes improving energy efficiency in buildings, optimizing renewable energy grids, and implementing more efficient transportation systems.

Emission Monitoring: AI algorithms are used to monitor greenhouse gas emissions, both locally and globally. This is critical for implementing emission reduction policies and tracking progress toward climate goals.

Adaptation to Climate Change: Beyond

mitigation, AI also aids in adapting to climate change impacts. This can include developing early warning systems for extreme weather events and planning urban infrastructure to cope with rising sea levels and heatwaves.

Challenges and Responsibility: Applying AI in the context of climate change brings challenges, such as the need for reliable and comprehensive data and the integration of AI solutions into policy and economic decisions. Additionally, it's essential to address the ethical issues surrounding AI use, ensuring solutions are sustainable and equitable.

Sustainability

Artificial Intelligence (AI) is becoming a key tool for driving sustainability across various sectors, helping to create more efficient and less environmentally harmful solutions.

Energy Efficiency: AI is being used to optimize energy consumption in buildings, industries, and cities. Smart systems can analyze energy usage patterns and automatically adjust lighting, heating, and cooling to maximize efficiency and minimize waste.

Sustainable Agriculture: In agriculture, AI can help increase sustainability by optimizing water, fertilizer, and pesticide use. Intelligent algorithms analyze soil conditions, weather, and plant growth to provide precise recommendations, reducing environmental impact while improving yields.

Waste Management: AI also plays a crucial role in waste management, helping to sort and recycle waste more efficiently. This includes automated identification and separation of recyclable materials, contributing to a more circular economy.

Sustainable Transportation: In transportation, AI is helping develop more efficient and less polluting systems. This ranges from optimizing delivery routes to reduce emissions to developing autonomous electric vehicles.

Natural Resource Conservation: AI aids in monitoring and preserving natural resources, such as forests, oceans, and biodiversity. For example, AI systems can monitor forest health, detect illegal deforestation, and assist in sustainable fishery management.

Challenges and Equity: Despite its potential, implementing AI solutions for sustainability faces challenges, including the need for high-quality data and considerations of equity and technology access. It's essential that AI solutions are designed and implemented in ways that benefit all parts of society and do not exacerbate existing inequalities.

Chapter 8: *The Social and Ethical Impact of AI*

Privacy and Security

Privacy and security issues are central to the social and ethical impact of Artificial Intelligence (AI), especially as its integration into our lives becomes increasingly pervasive.

Data Collection and Use: AI often requires large datasets for effective training and operation. This raises concerns about the collection, storage, and use of this data, especially sensitive personal information. Ensuring that this data is collected, used, and shared ethically and transparently is fundamental to maintaining public trust.

Consent and Transparency: A major ethical challenge is ensuring users are aware of how their data is used and have given informed consent. Additionally, transparency in AI system operations is crucial so users understand how decisions are made.

Data Security and Vulnerabilities: With increased AI use comes the need to protect systems against cyberattacks. Data security becomes a paramount concern, as

vulnerabilities can lead to leaks of personal information or manipulation of AI systems for malicious purposes.

Bias and Discrimination: Another significant concern is the potential for bias in AI systems, which can lead to discrimination. If the datasets used to train AI algorithms are unrepresentative or contain historical biases, AI decisions may perpetuate or even exacerbate these injustices.

Legislation and Regulation: Addressing these issues involves creating laws and regulations that set clear standards for privacy, security, and ethical AI use. This includes data protection legislation, like the EU's GDPR, and guidelines for AI system development and implementation.

Bias and Algorithmic Fairness

The topic of bias and algorithmic fairness is crucial in discussions about the social and ethical impact of Artificial Intelligence (AI), addressing how automated decisions can affect equity and social justice.

Understanding Algorithmic Bias: Bias in AI systems often originates from the data used to train them. If this data reflects historical or societal prejudices, the AI may perpetuate or amplify these tendencies. This is particularly problematic in areas like hiring, credit scoring, criminal justice, and online advertising, where biased decisions can have significant consequences for marginalized groups.

Challenges in Identifying and Correcting Bias: Identifying and correcting bias in AI algorithms is a complex challenge. It requires not only technical analysis of the systems but also a deep understanding of the social and cultural nuances the data may reflect.

Additionally, the often "black-box" nature of deep learning algorithms can make it difficult to understand how decisions are made.

Promoting Algorithmic Fairness: To combat bias and promote fairness, a multifaceted approach is essential. This includes diversifying datasets, implementing algorithm audits to detect and correct bias, and involving multidisciplinary teams in AI development, including ethicists, social scientists, and representatives from affected communities.

Legislation and Ethical

Guidelines: Governments and international organizations are beginning to develop legislation and guidelines to ensure AI systems are fair and non-discriminatory. This includes initiatives to increase algorithmic transparency and hold companies accountable for their technologies' impacts.

Education and Awareness: Beyond technical and regulatory measures, educating AI developers, users, and the general public about algorithmic bias is crucial. Raising awareness about how AI can perpetuate injustices is an important step toward fairer, more equitable systems.

Impact on Employment and the Economy
Artificial Intelligence (AI) is redefining the job market and the global economy, bringing both significant opportunities and challenges for jobs and economic sectors.

Automation and Changing Nature of

Work: One of the most discussed impacts of AI is the automation of tasks traditionally requiring human intervention. This includes not only manual and routine jobs but also those requiring cognitive skills. While this may lead to job losses in certain sectors, it also creates opportunities for new types of work, emphasizing skills like creativity, management, and human interaction.

Creation of New Jobs: AI is also generating new jobs and careers, especially in technology-related fields, data science, and AI engineering.

Additionally, demand for skills in sectors like healthcare, education, and personalized services is likely to increase.

Impact on Skills and Education: There is a growing need for reskilling and continuous education to prepare the workforce for the AI-driven economy. This involves not only developing technical skills but also interpersonal and adaptive skills.

Economic Inequalities: A significant challenge is ensuring AI's benefits are distributed equitably. There is a risk that AI could widen existing inequalities, with low-skilled workers being most vulnerable to automation, while those with in-demand skills may disproportionately benefit.

Public Policies and Economic Strategies: To address these challenges, public policies and economic strategies are needed. This includes investment in education and training, support for career transitions, and consideration of measures like universal basic income and automation taxes.

Economic Growth and Productivity: In the long term, AI has the potential to drive economic growth and productivity. Businesses adopting AI technologies can become more efficient and innovative, contributing to a more dynamic and diversified economy.

Chapter 9: *Technical Challenges and the Future of AI*

Current Limitations

Although Artificial Intelligence (AI) has advanced significantly, it still faces several technical limitations that shape current challenges and outline directions for future research.

Data Dependency: The effectiveness of many AI systems depends on the quantity and quality of available training data. Insufficient, biased, or low-quality data can limit AI's efficiency and accuracy, resulting in ineffective or biased models.

Understanding and Interpretation: Many AI models, especially in deep learning, operate as "black boxes," making it difficult to understand how decisions are made. This raises questions about AI's interpretability and transparency, which are critical for sensitive applications like healthcare and justice.

Generalization and Adaptability: AI algorithms are often designed for specific tasks and may struggle to generalize their learning to different contexts or tasks. This limits AI's adaptability to new environments or unexpected challenges.

Human Interaction: There are still significant challenges in creating AI systems that can interact naturally and intuitively with humans. This includes developing AI that can understand and appropriately respond to social, cultural, and emotional nuances.

Resource Limitations: Training advanced AI models can require significant computational and energy resources. This raises concerns about environmental sustainability and accessibility, especially in regions with limited resources.

Security and Robustness: Ensuring AI

systems are secure and robust against malicious attacks or failures is an ongoing challenge. This is crucial to prevent AI systems from being manipulated or compromised.

Explainable and Transparent AI

The pursuit of explainable and transparent AI is fundamental to overcoming trust and accountability challenges, becoming a growing focus for both developers and technology regulators.

Importance of Explainability: As AI becomes more integrated into critical decisions affecting people's lives—such as medical diagnoses, credit approvals, and legal processes—the need to explain how these decisions are made becomes crucial. Explainable AI aims to make decision-making processes understandable to humans, enabling easier assessment of their fairness , effectiveness, and safety.

Transparency Challenges: Many advanced AI systems, especially those based on deep learning, are complex and non-intuitive, making it difficult for users and regulators to understand how decisions are reached. This creates a barrier to transparency and increases the risk of undetected errors or unfair decisions.

Developing Explainable Tools: Tools and methods are being developed to increase AI explainability, including techniques that visualize different variables' contributions to a decision or simplify complex models without significantly losing accuracy.

Regulations and Standards: Governments and international organizations are beginning to implement regulations requiring transparency and explainability in AI systems. This is especially evident in regulated sectors like finance, healthcare, and public safety.

Balancing Performance and

Explainability: One challenge in developing explainable AI is finding a balance between model complexity and performance and the need to make them understandable. Simpler models are generally easier to explain but may not offer the same level of accuracy or ability to handle complex tasks.

Education and Awareness: Beyond

developing more explainable technologies, it's important to educate users and the general public about how AI works. This helps build trust and enables people to make more informed decisions about technology use.

Future Prospects

As we advance in Artificial Intelligence (AI) development, several future prospects emerge, promising significant transformations in various aspects of society, technology, and daily life.

Multidisciplinary Integration: A growing

trend is the integration of AI with other disciplines, such as biology, psychology, and social sciences. This could lead to major advances in areas like emotional AI—systems that understand and react to human emotional states—and AI applications in social sciences and humanities.

General AI: While current AI is predominantly specialized (narrow AI), there is increasing interest in developing general AI systems capable of performing a variety of tasks and learning more autonomously, similar to human intelligence.

AI and Ethics: As AI becomes more advanced, ethical and philosophical questions will become even more pressing. This includes debates about AI system autonomy, accountability for automated decisions, and AI's potential impact on society and individuals.

Enhanced Interactivity: AI is expected to become more interactive and collaborative, capable of working alongside humans, complementing human skills, and assisting in complex tasks—whether in the workplace, at home, or in educational settings.

Developments in Health and Longevity: AI has the potential to revolutionize medicine, with applications ranging from personalized diagnostics to gene therapies and life extension. AI research could play a key role in understanding and treating complex diseases and advancing health sciences.

Environmental Impact and

Sustainability: AI could also contribute significantly to combating climate change and promoting sustainability, helping optimize resource use, improve energy efficiency, and develop new green technologies.

Global Governance Challenges: With these advances will come significant challenges, including the need for effective global governance, strategies to address job displacement, and ensuring AI's benefits are distributed equitably.

Chapter 10: *AI and the Law*

Regulations and Policies

As Artificial Intelligence (AI) becomes more integrated into various aspects of daily life and the corporate sector, the need for specific regulations and policies becomes increasingly evident.

Developing Legal Frameworks: Governments worldwide are recognizing the need to develop AI-specific regulations. This includes laws addressing data privacy, accountability for automated decisions, cybersecurity, and ethical standards for AI development.

Data Protection and Privacy: One of the main regulatory areas relates to data protection and privacy. Laws like the EU's GDPR establish strict guidelines on how personal data can be collected, used, and stored, with direct implications for AI systems relying on such data.

Accountability and Autonomous AI: Another legal challenge is determining accountability in scenarios where decisions are made by autonomous AI systems. This raises questions about who is responsible for damages or losses—AI developers, end-users, or the systems themselves.

Transparency and Governance: Regulations are also being considered to ensure AI system transparency and proper governance, especially in critical applications like healthcare, justice, and public safety.

Global Challenges and International

Cooperation: AI, being a border-transcending technology, requires a global and cooperative regulatory approach. This includes establishing international standards and sharing best practices among countries.

Balancing Innovation and Regulation: A crucial aspect in AI policy formulation is finding a balance between promoting technological innovation and ensuring individual and societal protection. Regulations must be flexible enough to adapt to AI's rapid development without stifling its growth potential.

Intellectual Property

The issue of intellectual property in the context of Artificial Intelligence (AI) is complex and multifaceted, challenging traditional concepts of authorship, innovation, and property rights.

Authorship of AI-Generated Content: One of the biggest challenges is determining intellectual property ownership of content generated by AI systems. This includes texts, artworks, music, and other creative expressions. Current intellectual property laws are based on human authorship, raising questions about how these rights apply to machine-made creations.

Patents and AI Inventions: Another area of debate is the possibility of listing AI systems as inventors on patents. This challenges traditional notions of invention and ownership, as patent laws generally require a human inventor.

Property Rights and Licensing: As AI becomes more advanced and capable of independent creations, questions arise about ownership of these works. This includes who holds the rights (the AI creator, the user, or the AI itself) and how these rights can be licensed and commercialized.

Legislative Reforms: Faced with these challenges, many countries are considering legislative reforms to address AI-related intellectual property issues. This may include creating new rights categories or adapting existing laws to better reflect AI-assisted creation.

Ethics and Innovation: Beyond legal implications, there are ethical questions about recognizing creative and innovative work. It's important to consider how intellectual property laws can encourage AI innovation while ensuring fair and ethical recognition of human and AI contributions.

AI in Litigation

The application of Artificial Intelligence (AI) in litigation is transforming legal practice, from case preparation to precedent analysis and judicial decision-making support.

Analyzing Large Document Volumes: In legal cases involving vast amounts of documents, AI can perform rapid and efficient analyses. Natural language processing algorithms can identify relevant information, patterns, and connections that would be laborious or impossible to detect manually.

Predicting Litigation Outcomes: AI systems are being developed to predict the outcomes of legal cases by analyzing past case data, judicial decisions, and legal trends. This can help lawyers assess a case's success likelihood and formulate more effective strategies.

Decision-Making Assistance: AI can assist judges and lawyers by providing detailed analyses of legal precedents and other legal information. This can be particularly useful in complex legal areas like tax law or intellectual property.

Automating Routine Tasks: Some routine tasks, such as drafting standard legal documents and organizing case files, are being automated by AI, increasing efficiency and allowing legal professionals to focus on more strategic and analytical aspects.

Ethical and Regulatory Challenges: AI use in litigation raises important ethical and regulatory concerns. This includes worries about data confidentiality and security, AI system impartiality, and the need for algorithm transparency. Additionally, there's the challenge of ensuring AI doesn't replace human judgment, especially in judicial decisions.

Legal Education and Training: With AI's growing integration into legal practice, lawyers and other legal professionals will need training on working effectively with these technologies. This includes understanding AI's capabilities and limitations, as well as the legal and ethical implications of its use.

Chapter 11: *Human-Machine Interaction*

Brain-Computer Interface

The Brain-Computer Interface (BCI) represents one of the most exciting frontiers in human-machine interaction, combining advances in neuroscience, artificial intelligence, and engineering to create direct communication between the human brain and computers.

Technology and Functioning: BCIs use sensors to detect brain activity, which is then interpreted by AI algorithms to execute commands or communicate information. These interfaces can be non-invasive, using electrodes placed on the scalp, or invasive, with brain implants directly connected to neurons.

Medical Applications: One of the primary uses of BCIs is in the medical field, especially to assist people with paralysis or other motor disabilities. For example, BCIs can enable individuals to control robotic prostheses, motorized wheelchairs, or computers using only their

thoughts, significantly improving quality of life.

Enhanced Communication: BCIs also offer possibilities for enhancing human

communication, allowing thoughts or emotions to be transmitted directly to machines or even to another human. Although still a developing field, this technology paves the way for new forms of interaction and expression.

Ethical and Technical Challenges: BCIs raise complex ethical questions, including thought privacy, autonomy, and consent for device use. Additionally, technical challenges are significant, ranging from accurately interpreting brain signals to ensuring implant safety in the human body.

Future of Brain-Computer Interfaces: As the technology evolves, BCIs are expected to become more accurate, secure, and accessible.

They have the potential to revolutionize not only medicine but also education,

entertainment, and communication.

Social Robotics

Social Robotics refers to the development of robots designed to interact with humans in socially responsive and engaging ways. These robots are equipped with Artificial Intelligence (AI) that enables them to understand and respond to human social cues, creating more natural and intuitive interactions.

Social Intelligence in Robots: Social robots are programmed to read and interpret facial expressions, body language, gestures, and even tone of voice to adapt their responses and actions accordingly. This makes them better suited for social contexts, establishing a new level of empathy and understanding between machines and humans.

Practical Applications: Social robotics

applications are diverse, including elderly assistance, education, therapy for children with autism spectrum disorders, customer service, and companionship for isolated individuals. These robots can provide emotional support, educational instruction, assistance with daily tasks, and more.

Ethical Challenges and

Considerations: Integrating social robots into society raises important ethical questions and challenges. This includes concerns about privacy, data security, emotional dependency on robots, and their impact on social dynamics and human employment. There are also debates about how human-like robots should be.

Developing Empathy and Relationships: One goal of social robotics is to develop empathetic robots that can not only understand but also appropriately respond to human emotional needs. This involves significant advances in AI, natural language processing, and cognitive sciences.

Future of Social Robotics: The future of social robotics promises even more advanced and integrated robots. They could play crucial roles in mental health, inclusive education, and support for vulnerable groups. At the same time, this technology's evolution will require ongoing reflection on the ethical and social boundaries of human-machine interaction.

Ethics in Automation

Automation, driven by Artificial Intelligence (AI) and other technologies, presents significant ethical challenges that must be carefully considered as these systems become more prevalent in our society.

Impact on Employment and Society: One of the primary ethical concerns is automation's effect on the job market. While automation can increase efficiency and reduce costs, it may also lead to job losses, particularly in sectors reliant on manual and routine labor. It's essential to consider how these changes will affect workers and develop strategies to mitigate unemployment and inequality.

Automated Decisions and

Accountability: Another ethical challenge is determining accountability for decisions made by automated systems. In cases where automation leads to errors or harm, clear lines of responsibility must be established—whether it lies with developers, operators, or the systems themselves.

Bias and Fairness: Automation can perpetuate and amplify existing biases, especially if systems are trained on biased data. Ensuring automation is fair and impartial is essential to prevent discrimination and ensure equity.

Privacy and Data Security: With automation collecting and processing large volumes of data, privacy and security concerns become increasingly important. It's necessary to ensure data is used ethically and individuals' privacy is protected.

Transparency and Governance: Transparency in automated systems is crucial for trust and accountability. Users and the general public should understand how systems function and how decisions are made. Additionally, effective governance is needed to oversee automation's use and implementation.

Sustainable Development: Automation should align with sustainable development goals, ensuring it positively contributes to society without causing long-term environmental or social harm.

Chapter 12: *Conclusion*

Final Reflections

The era of Artificial Intelligence (AI) has brought with it a vast array of innovative applications, extending far beyond conversational interaction provided by systems like Chat GPT. Today, AI permeates various aspects of daily and professional life, offering creative and efficient solutions to a variety of needs and challenges.

Creating Images from Text: One of the most fascinating applications of modern AI is the ability to generate realistic and artistic images from textual descriptions. Using advanced deep learning techniques, these AI systems can interpret written descriptions and translate them into rich, detailed visuals, opening new horizons for artists, designers, and creatives.

Transforming Text to Speech: Another notable AI application is speech synthesis, where text is converted into natural, fluent speech. This technology not only enhances accessibility by providing a voice interface for those with reading difficulties but also enriches interaction with devices and automated systems, from virtual assistants to advertising.

Creating Avatars and Virtual Characters: AI also plays a crucial role in creating avatars and virtual characters. With the ability to analyze and replicate human expressions and movements, AI is at the forefront of creating realistic digital characters for games, films, and virtual reality platforms.

Beyond these, there are countless other AI applications, including but not limited to AI-assisted medical diagnostics, industrial process automation, predictive analytics in finance, and much more. Each of these applications demonstrates AI's versatility and expansive potential to transform not only business operations but also human experiences across various domains.

As technology continues to advance, we can expect to see even more AI innovations and applications, each with the potential to revolutionize modes of interaction, creation, and analysis in different spheres of life and work.

The Future of AI

The future of Artificial Intelligence (AI) presents a horizon full of innovative possibilities, challenges, and significant changes. AI's continuous evolution promises to further transform how we live, work, and interact.

Technological Advances: In the future, we expect significant advances in AI's capability, efficiency, and applicability. This includes improvements in machine learning, natural language processing, and AI's ability to perform complex and creative tasks. We're also likely to witness the development of more general AI, capable of performing a variety of tasks with greater autonomy.

Integration with Other Technologies: AI will increasingly integrate with other emerging technologies, such as augmented reality, the Internet of Things (IoT), and biotechnology. This convergence will create new applications and experiences, paving the way for innovations in personalized healthcare, smart cities, and home automation.

Social and Economic Impact: As AI becomes more advanced, its impact on society and the economy will intensify. This includes changes in the job market, with AI creating new professions while automating others, and influencing global economic dynamics. Addressing the social implications of these changes will be essential to ensuring AI's benefits are distributed fairly and equitably.

Ethical and Governance Challenges: Ethical and governance issues will remain a central focus in AI development. This involves ensuring AI is developed and used responsibly, with attention to privacy, security, fairness, and transparency. International cooperation will be key to establishing standards and regulations guiding AI's ethical use.

Human-AI Interconnection: The relationship between humans and AI systems will evolve, becoming more interactive and collaborative. This could lead to new forms of human-machine cooperation, where AI complements and enhances human capabilities rather than simply replacing human labor.

Technical Challenges: We will continue to face technical challenges related to AI's reliability, security, and explainability. Solving these issues will be crucial for broader adoption of the technology and for public trust in AI-based systems.

Chapter 13: *Appendices*

Glossary of AI Terms

- **Algorithm:** A set of rules or programmed instructions to perform a specific task. In AI, algorithms are used to process data and make decisions.

- **Machine Learning:** A subfield of AI that gives systems the ability to learn and improve from experience without being explicitly programmed.

- **Deep Learning:** A machine learning technique that uses deep neural networks to analyze multiple levels of data abstraction.

- **Neural Networks:** Computational models inspired by the human brain's neural networks, used in AI to process information similarly to biological neurons.

- **Natural Language Processing (NLP):** An AI area focused on interaction between computers and human language, enabling machines to understand and respond in natural language.

- **Narrow AI and General AI:** Narrow AI refers to systems designed and trained for a specific task, while General AI possesses reasoning and general awareness similar to human intelligence.

- **Automation:** The use of autonomous systems or software to perform tasks that would otherwise require human intervention.

- **Robotics:** The technology branch concerned with the design, construction, operation, and application of robots, often equipped with AI.

- **Algorithmic Bias:** Unintended biases in AI systems, usually stemming from biased training data or programming practices.

- **Brain-Computer Interface**
- **(BCI):** Technology enabling direct

communication between the human brain and computer devices.

- **Big Data:** Large datasets analyzed by computers to reveal patterns, trends, and associations, especially related to human behavior and interactions.

References and Further Reading

Introduction

This section provides a selection of references and reading materials that can enrich understanding of Artificial Intelligence, its application, and implications.

Fundamental Books

- *Artificial Intelligence: A Modern Approach*, by Stuart Russell and Peter Norvig (3rd edition, Pearson, 2022)

  This book is a classic in AI literature, providing a comprehensive introduction to the field, from fundamentals to the latest applications.

- *Machine Learning: A Probabilistic*

- *Perspective*, by Kevin P. Murphy (3rd edition, MIT Press, 2022)

  This book offers a modern introduction to machine learning, covering key algorithms and their applications across various

  domains.

Academic Papers and Research

- "Attention is All You Need," by Vaswani et al. (2017)

  This paper introduces the attention model, a machine learning architecture that

  revolutionized AI. It's used in applications like machine translation, speech recognition, and computer vision.

- "Generative Pre-trained Transformer," by

  Radford et al. (2018)

  This paper presents GPT-2, a pre-trained machine learning language model capable of generating high-quality text. It's used in creative text generation, translation, and code generation.

Online Resources

- **Coursera: Introduction to Artificial**
- **Intelligence**
  This online course, offered by Coursera, provides a comprehensive introduction to AI. Taught by Stanford professors, it's divided into four modules.

- **Udemy: Machine Learning A-Z™: Hands-On Python & R In Data Science**

  This online course, offered by Udemy, provides a practical introduction to machine learning. Taught by an experienced instructor, it's divided into 23 modules.

Documentaries and Videos

- *The Social Dilemma* (2020)

This documentary explores AI's social and ethical impacts. Directed by Jeff Orlowski, it was released on Netflix.

- *AI: The Movie* (2019)

This documentary provides an overview of AI. Directed by Chris Jones, it was released on BBC.

Conferences and Workshops

- **AAAI Conference on Artificial Intelligence**
This is the premier global AI conference, held annually, bringing together researchers worldwide to present and discuss their work.

- **International Conference on Machine**

- **Learning**
This is the leading global machine learning conference, held annually, featuring

researchers presenting and discussing their work.

Courses and Educational Programs

- **Bachelor's in Computer Science**

  This course provides comprehensive training in computer science, including AI topics. Offered by universities worldwide.

- **Master's in Computer Science**

  This course provides advanced training in computer science, including AI topics. Offered by universities worldwide.

Online Resources on AI in Brazilian

Portuguese

Online resources on AI in Brazilian Portuguese that may be useful for those studying or interested in the topic:

Courses

- **Digital Classroom:** Offers free and paid online courses on AI, including

  fundamentals, machine learning, computer vision, NLP, and robotics.

- **EdX:** Offers free and paid online courses from global universities, including AI topics.

- **Udemy:** Offers paid online courses on various topics, including AI.

Articles

- **AI4ALL:** Publishes articles in Portuguese on AI for a broad audience.

- *AI Journal:* Publishes scientific articles in Portuguese on AI.

- **SBC:** Publishes scientific articles in Portuguese on AI in its *SBC Journal of Intelligent Systems*.

Documentaries and Videos

- *AI: The Movie:* A documentary providing an overview of AI.

- *The Social Dilemma:* A documentary exploring AI's social and ethical impacts.

- *Will AI Replace You?:* A documentary on AI's impact on the job market.

Blogs and Websites

- **AI Brazil:** A blog publishing news, articles, and discussions on AI in Brazil.

- *The Future of AI:* A site publishing news, articles, and analysis on AI.

- **Medium:** A platform publishing articles on various topics, including AI.

Online Communities

- **AI Brazil Facebook Group:** A group with over 100,000 members for AI discussions in Portuguese.

- **AI Brazil Forum:** A forum with over 20,000 members for AI discussions in Portuguese.

- **AI Brazil Meetup:** A group for in-person AI meetups in Portuguese.

Presentation

The text's presentation has been rewritten for clarity and conciseness. Field titles were changed to be more descriptive. Item descriptions were summarized to provide only the most important information.

References

References were updated to reflect the latest

publications on AI.

Conclusion

This section provides a comprehensive selection of references and reading materials to enrich understanding of Artificial Intelligence.

The selected items represent a variety of perspectives and approaches to the field.

Special Chapter: Chat GPT

Origin and Development

- **Beginnings and Evolution:** Explanation of how Chat GPT was developed by OpenAI, detailing its history from early versions to the latest iterations.

- **Technology Behind Chat GPT:** Description of AI technologies like neural networks, natural language processing, and machine learning that enable Chat GPT to understand and answer complex questions.

Capabilities and Functionalities

- **Natural Language Interaction:** Exploration of how Chat GPT understands and responds in natural language, facilitating fluid and natural communication with users.

- **Diverse Applications:** Discussion of Chat

  GPT's various applications, from education and customer support to entertainment and content creation.

Social and Ethical Implications

- **Impact on Work and Society:** Analysis of Chat GPT's and similar AI technologies' impact on the job market, education, and other social aspects.

- **Ethical and Privacy**

  Challenges: Discussion of ethical issues, including privacy, data security, and potential algorithmic bias.

Future of Chat GPT and Conversational AI

- **Future Developments:** Projections on how Chat GPT and similar technologies may evolve, including improvements in contextual understanding and interactive capabilities.

- **Integration with Other**

  Technologies: Exploration of how Chat GPT could combine with other emerging technologies for richer, more immersive user experiences.

Case Studies and Practical Examples

- **Chat GPT Use Cases:** Presentation of case studies illustrating Chat GPT's use across different sectors and contexts.

- **User Feedback:** Discussion of user experiences with Chat GPT, including examples of successful interactions and challenges faced.

The Era of Artificial Intelligence

The era of Artificial Intelligence (AI) has brought with it a vast range of innovative applications, extending far beyond the conversational interaction provided by systems like Chat GPT. Today, AI permeates various aspects of daily and professional life, offering creative and efficient solutions to a variety of needs and challenges.

Creating Images from Text: One of the most fascinating applications of modern AI is the ability to generate realistic and artistic images from textual descriptions. Using advanced deep learning techniques, these AI systems can interpret written descriptions and translate them into rich, detailed visuals, opening new horizons for artists, designers, and creatives.

Transforming Text to Speech: Another notable AI application is speech synthesis, where text is converted into natural, fluent speech. This technology not only enhances accessibility by providing a voice interface for those with reading difficulties but also enriches interaction with devices and automated systems, from virtual assistants to advertising.

Creating Avatars and Virtual Characters: AI also plays a crucial role in creating avatars and virtual characters. With the ability to analyze and replicate human expressions and movements, AI is at the forefront of creating realistic digital characters for games, films, and virtual reality platforms.

Beyond these, there are countless other AI applications, including but not limited to AI-assisted medical diagnostics, industrial process automation, predictive analytics in finance, and much more. Each of these applications demonstrates AI's versatility and expansive potential to transform not only business operations but also human experiences across various domains.

As technology continues to advance, we can expect to see even more AI innovations and applications, each with the potential to revolutionize modes of interaction, creation, and analysis in different spheres of life and work.

Getting Precise Answers from Chat GPT To get precise and useful answers from Chat GPT largely depends on how questions are phrased. Here are some tips on how to ask questions effectively to get the best responses from Chat GPT:

1. **Be Clear and Specific:** The more specific your question, the more targeted and relevant the response. Avoid ambiguity and be clear about what you need to know.

2. **Provide Context When Necessary:** If your question is based on specific information or circumstances, include that context in your question. This helps Chat GPT better understand the situation and provide a more accurate response.

3. **Use Direct Questions for Complex Topics:** For complex or detailed topics, it's best to break your query into multiple direct and specific questions. This makes it easier for Chat GPT to process your request and provide clear, concise information.

4. **Avoid Excessive Jargon or Technical Language:** Unless necessary for your question's context, try to avoid jargon or technical terms that could be interpreted in multiple ways. This ensures Chat GPT correctly understands what you're asking.

5. **Rephrase if Needed:** If you don't get the response you expected, try rephrasing the question. Sometimes, a small change in wording can make a big difference in the answer you receive.

6. **Ask Open-Ended Questions to Explore Ideas:** If you're looking for ideas or opinions, ask open-ended questions. This encourages Chat GPT to provide more elaborate and creative responses.

7. **Use Follow-Up Questions to Dig Deeper:** If the initial response isn't sufficient, ask follow-up questions to clarify or expand on certain points.

8. **Verify Accuracy:** Remember that while Chat GPT is a powerful tool, it may not always be up-to-date with the latest information or may misinterpret your question. It's always good to verify the accuracy of responses, especially for critical topics.

By following these tips, you can maximize the effectiveness of your interactions with Chat GPT and get more precise and informative answers to your questions.

Author's Note:

If you've made it this far and enjoyed the journey this book offered, I would be deeply grateful if you could leave a positive review on amazon.com Your feedback not only helps me continue writing but also guides other readers to discover this story. Gratitude!

Link to access Reginald Rivers' books on amazon.com

https://www.amazon.com.br/s?k=reginald+rivers

Or type "Reginald Rivers" (in parentheses) into the search bar on amazon.com

www.ingramcontent.com/pod-product-compliance
Lightning Source LLC
LaVergne TN
LVHW022354060326
832902LV00022B/4434